Big Sailor

My First Big ABC

Ages 3-5

Vol.6 P·Q·R

Eggadu!
Your study buddy

My First Big ABC Book Series
Big Sailor Edu

Copyright © 2021 Cambridge Dynasty Press

For permission requests, bulk order information, or any busine ss related inquiries, please contact the publisher at the email address below.

Cambridge Dynasty Press
30 N Gould St. STE4000
Sheridan, WY 82801
Email: Bestsailoredu@Gmail.com

Written, Designed, and Printed in the United States of America

978-1-7357844-6-5(Paperback)

47678459

Hi! Nice to meet you.
My name is Eggadu!

I am your study buddy
for this book!

1. Building Skills for Pen Control
2. Recognizing Alphabet Letters
3. Building Confidence
4. Enjoying a Good Book
5. Being Patient with Practice
6. Developing Creative Thinking
7. Being Proud of Achievement
8. Having Fun

This book belongs to

_____
(name)

Let's trace following the numbers

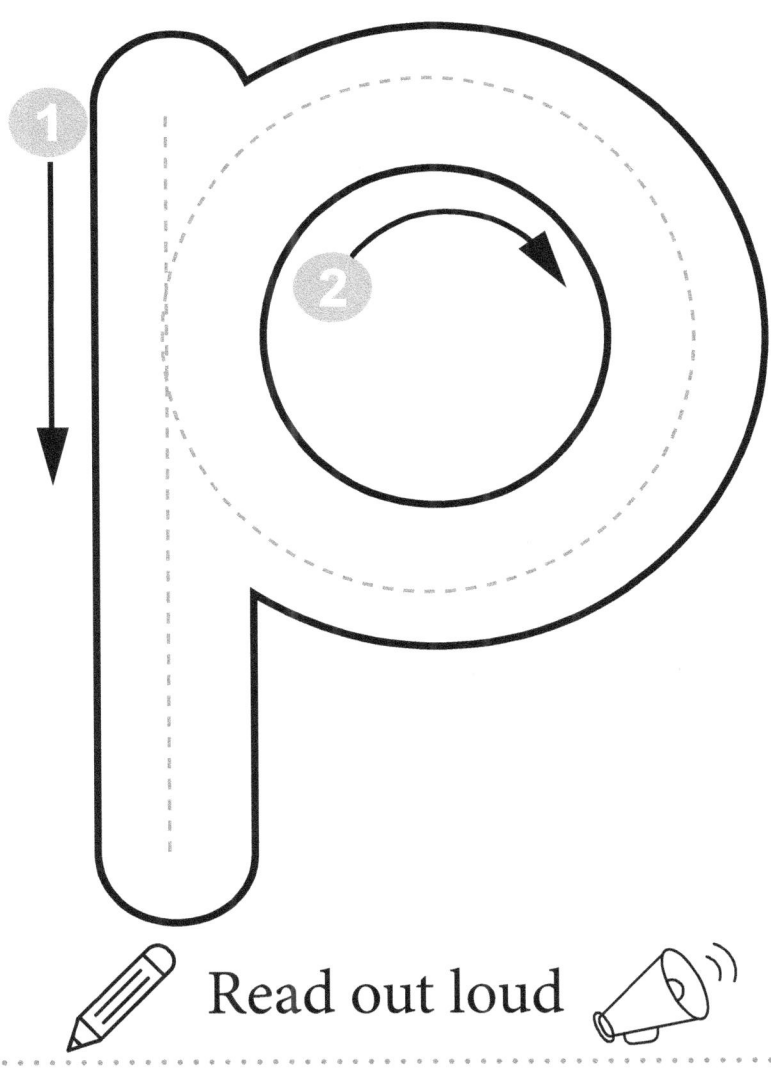

✏️ Read out loud 📣

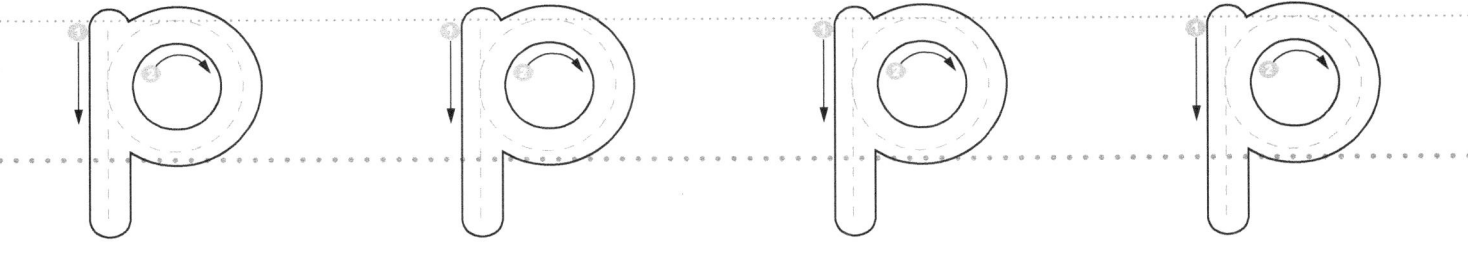

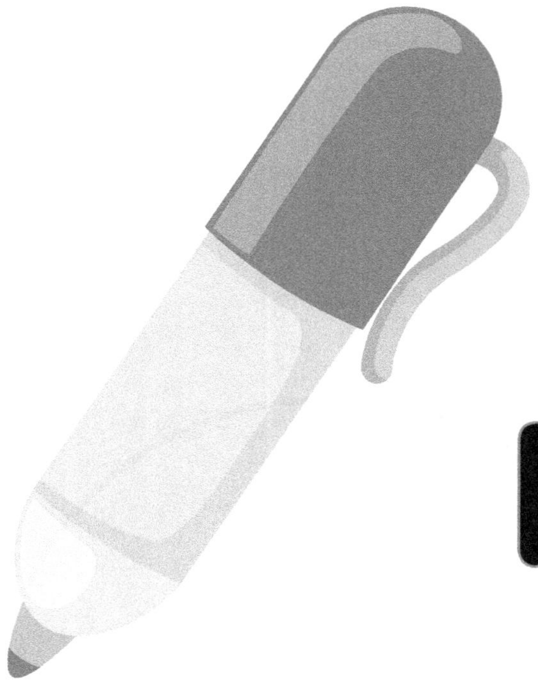

Pen

✏️ Let's trace following the numbers 📣

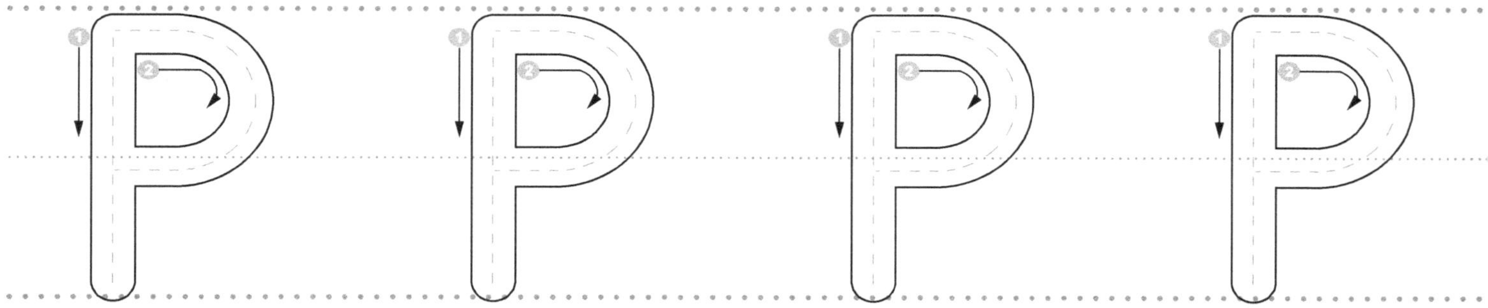

P P P P

Pumpkin

penquin

✏️ Read out loud 📣

p   p   p   p

pig

Find every P and color them

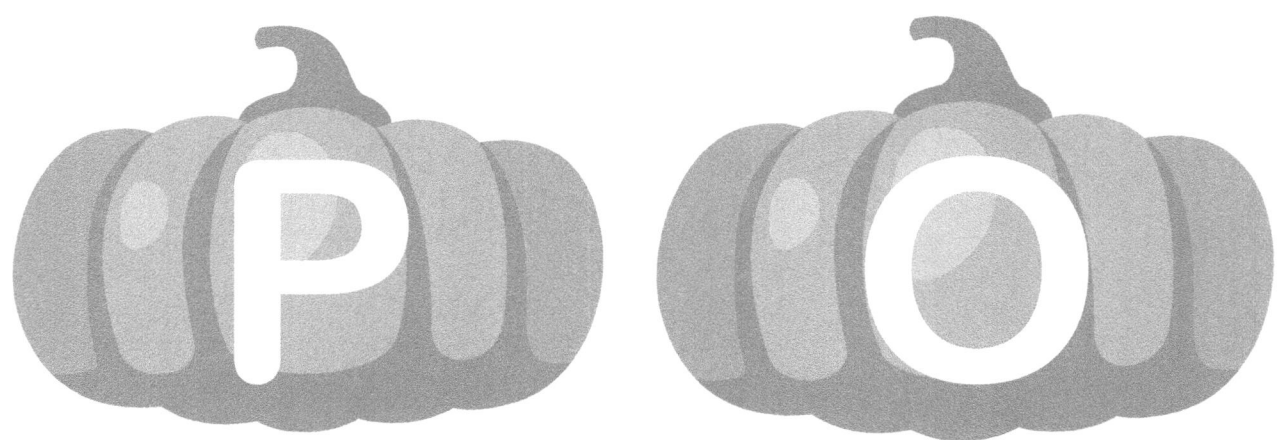

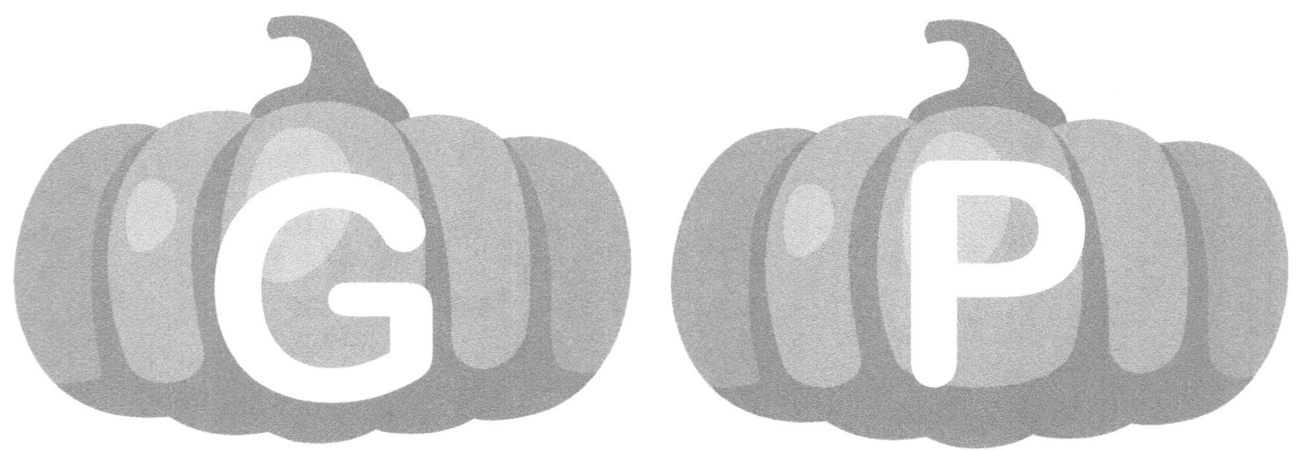

Trace the dotted line and read out loud

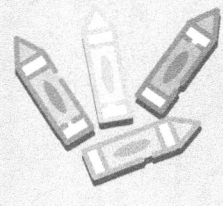 **Find every P and color the sections**

Eggadu

Trace the dotted line and read out loud

15

p for penguin

Draw lines to match

 # Find every p and color the sections

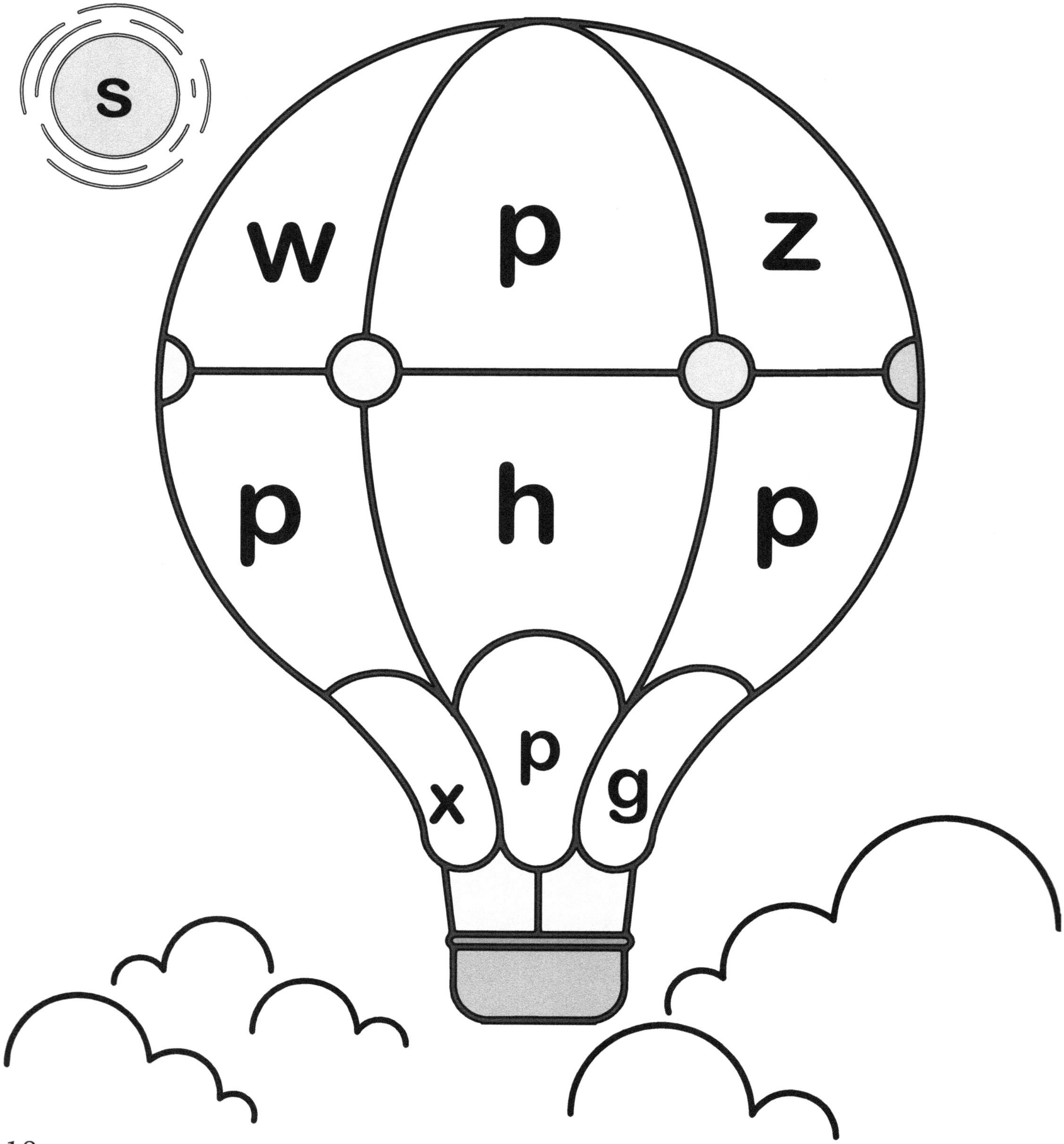

Trace the dotted line and read out loud

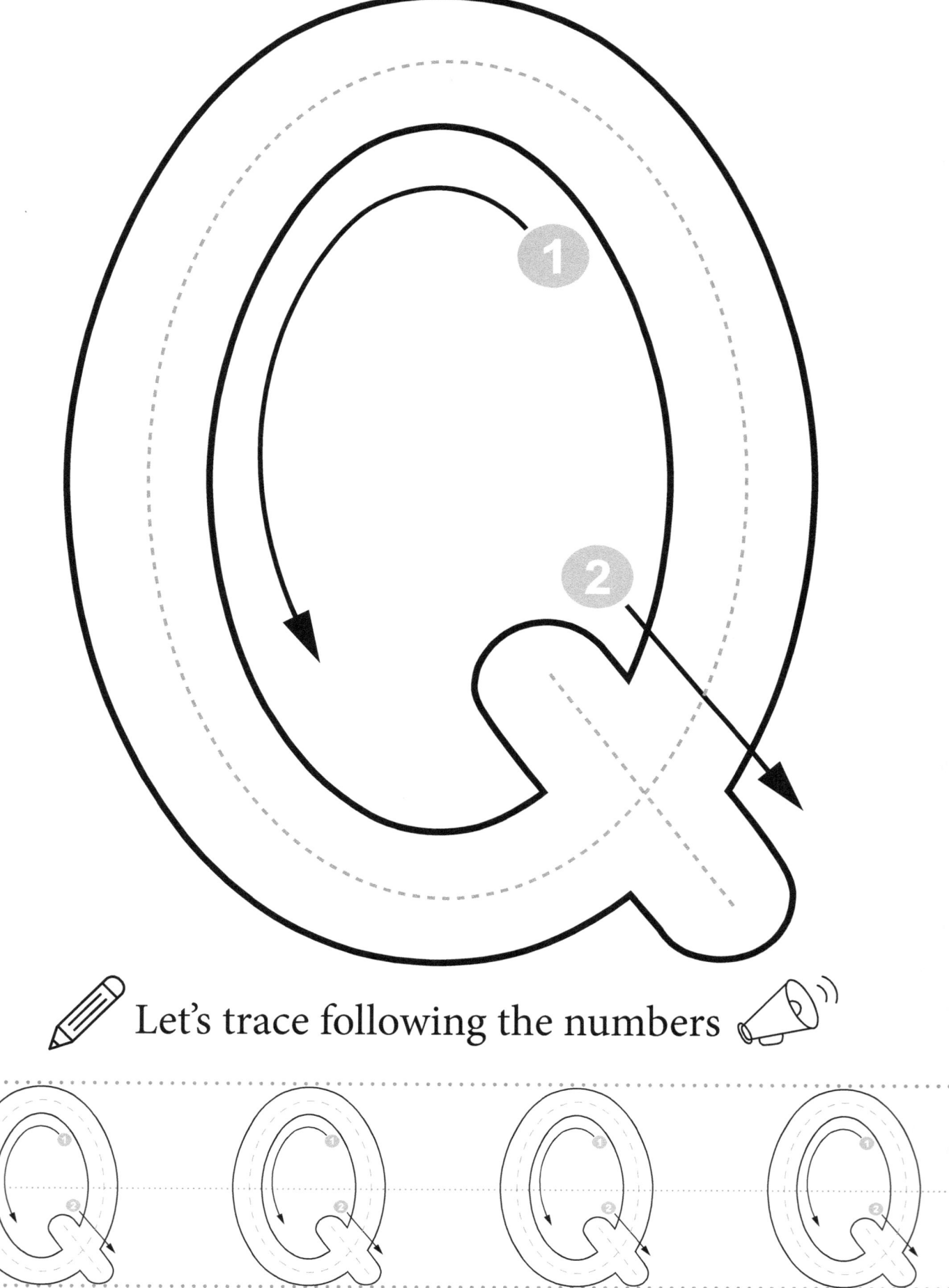

Let's trace following the numbers

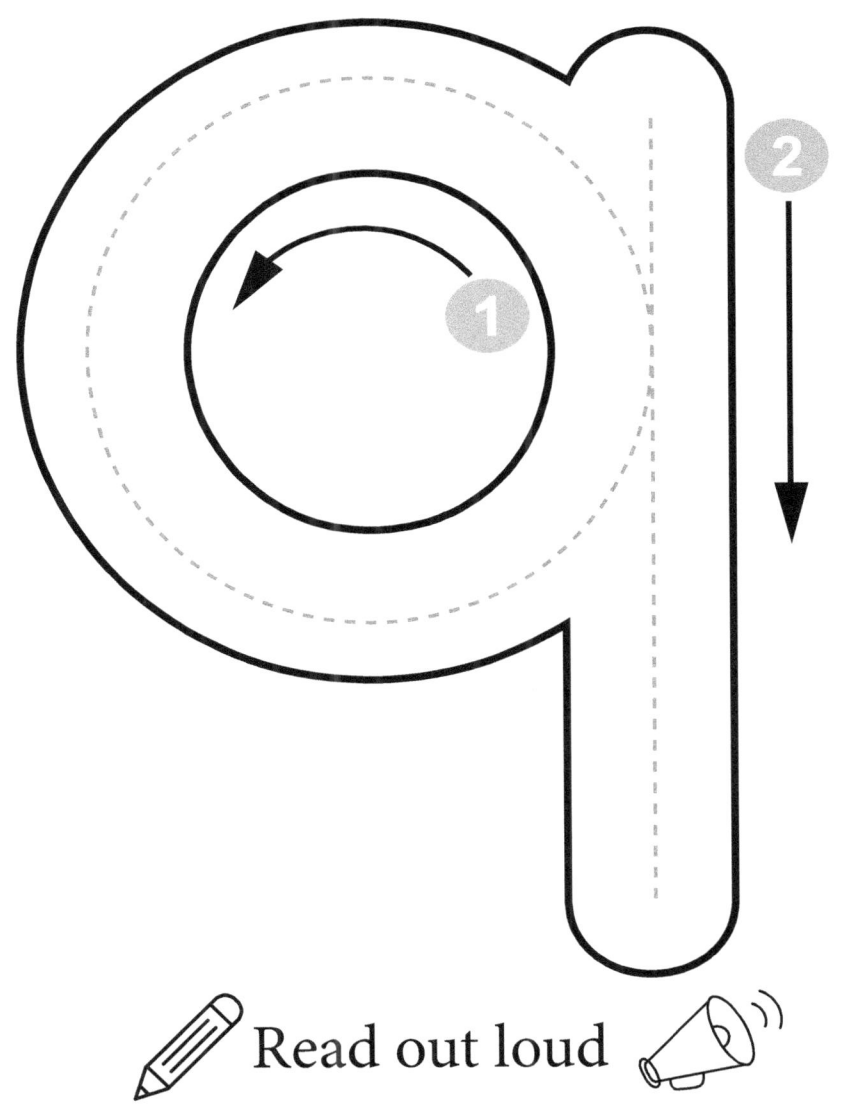

✏️ Read out loud 📣

Quince

 Let's trace following the numbers

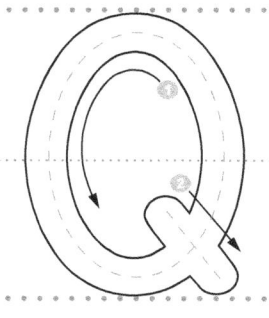 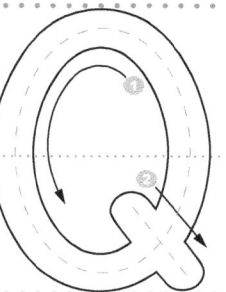 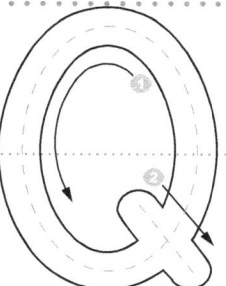 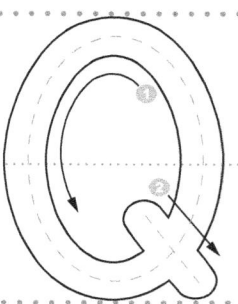

Quail

quill

 Read out loud

 # quiver

Find every Q and color them

Trace the dotted line and read out loud

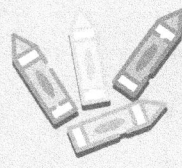 **Find every Q and color the sections**

Eggadu

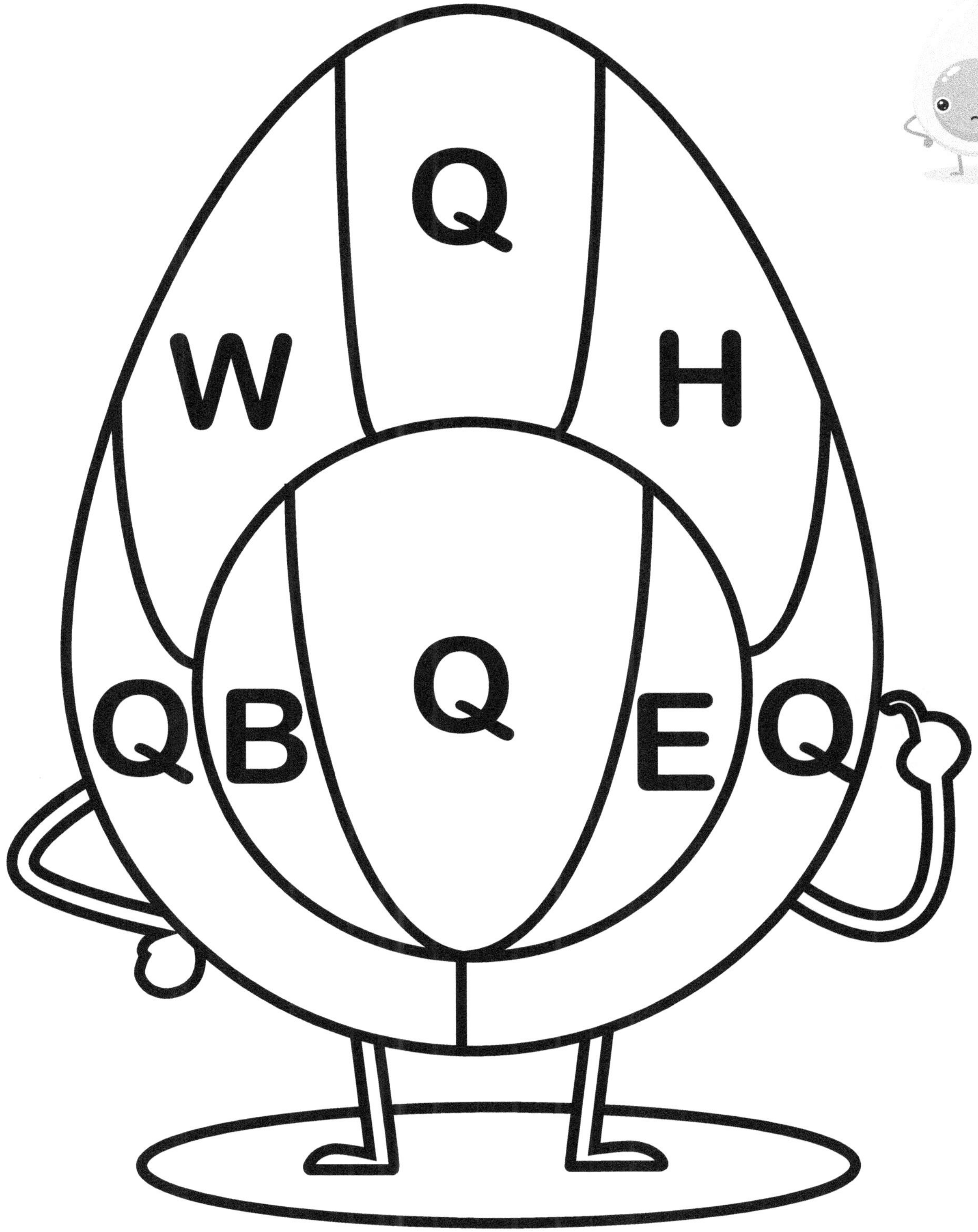

Find every q and circle them

q for quill

Trace the dotted line and read out loud

Draw lines to match

q for quail

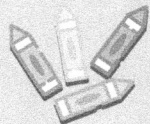 # Find every q and color the sections

Trace the dotted line and read out loud

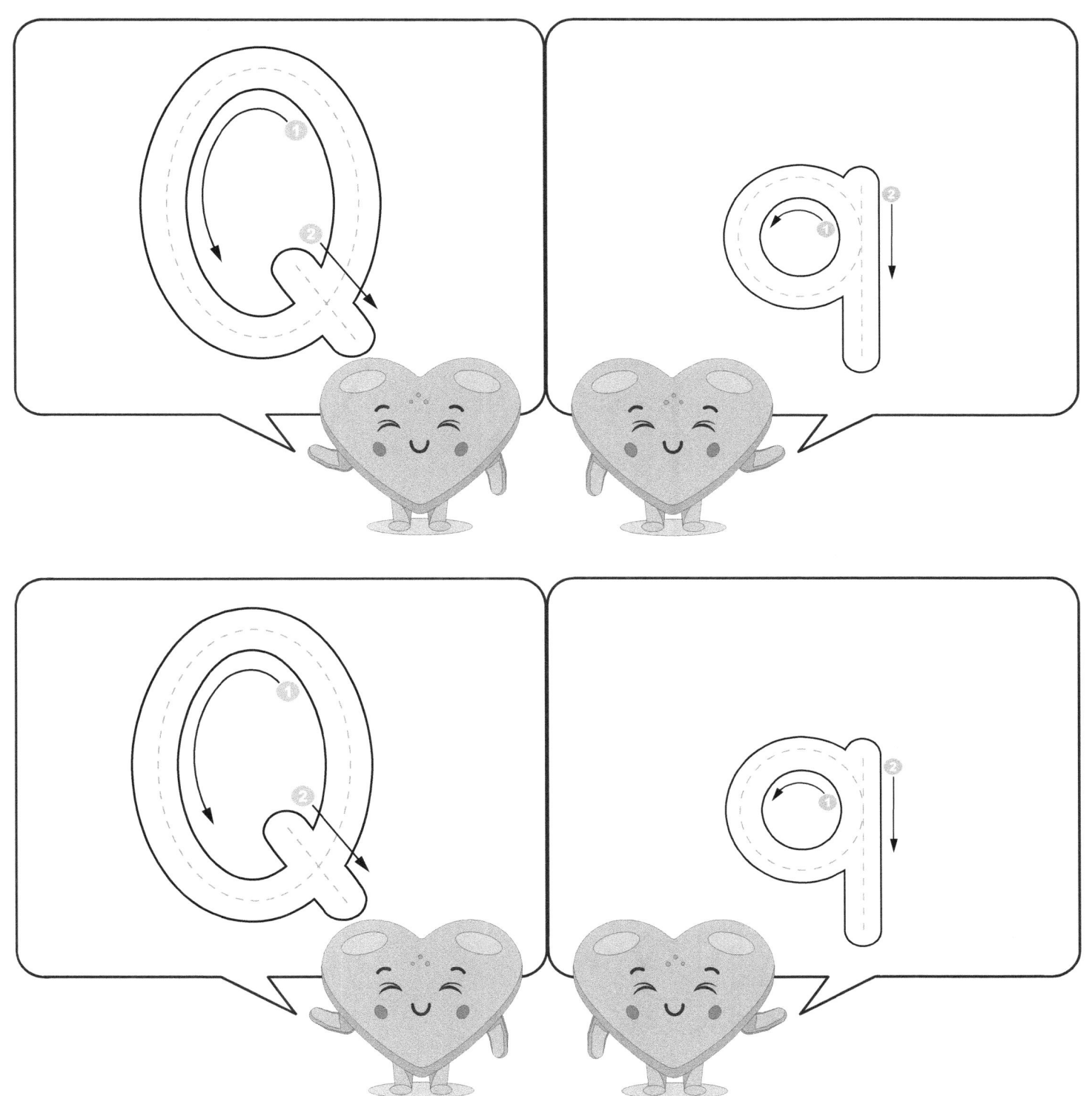

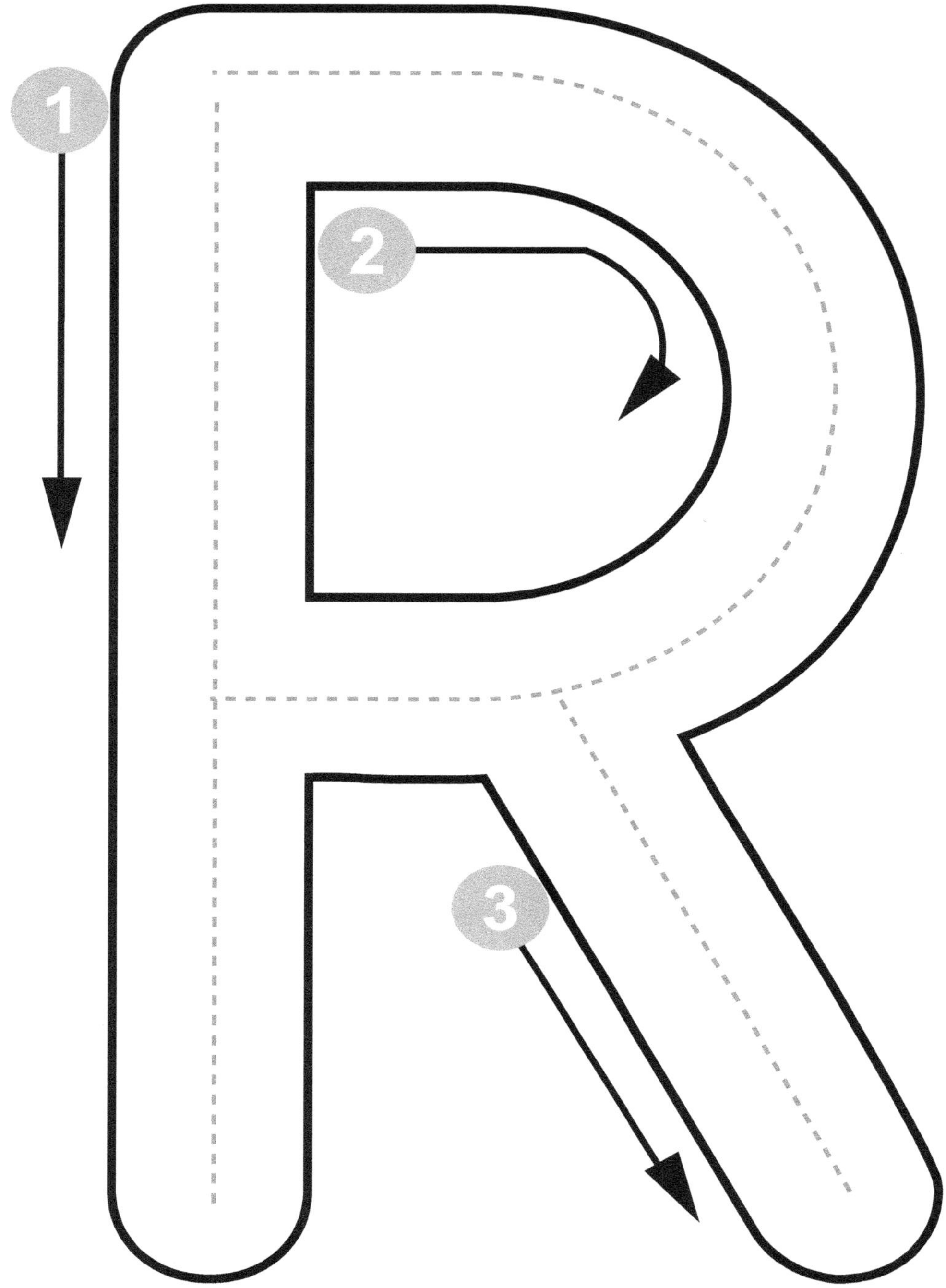

 Let's trace following the numbers

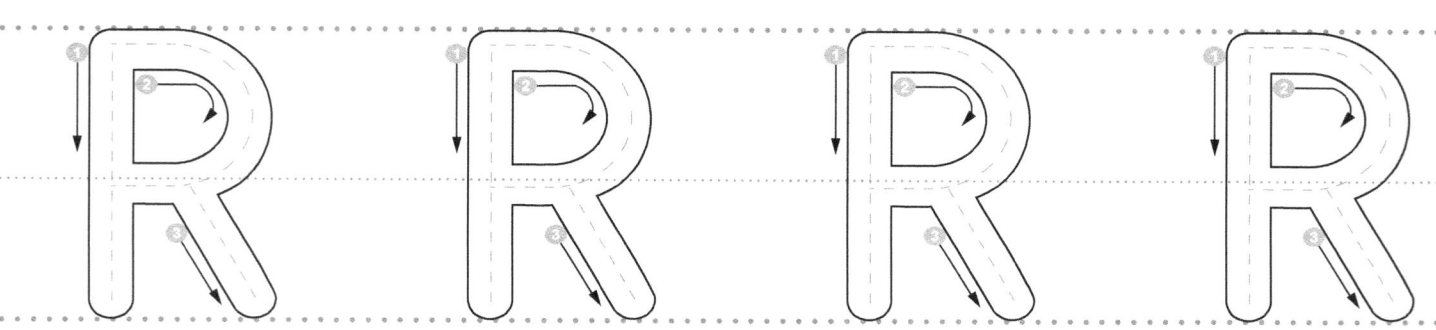

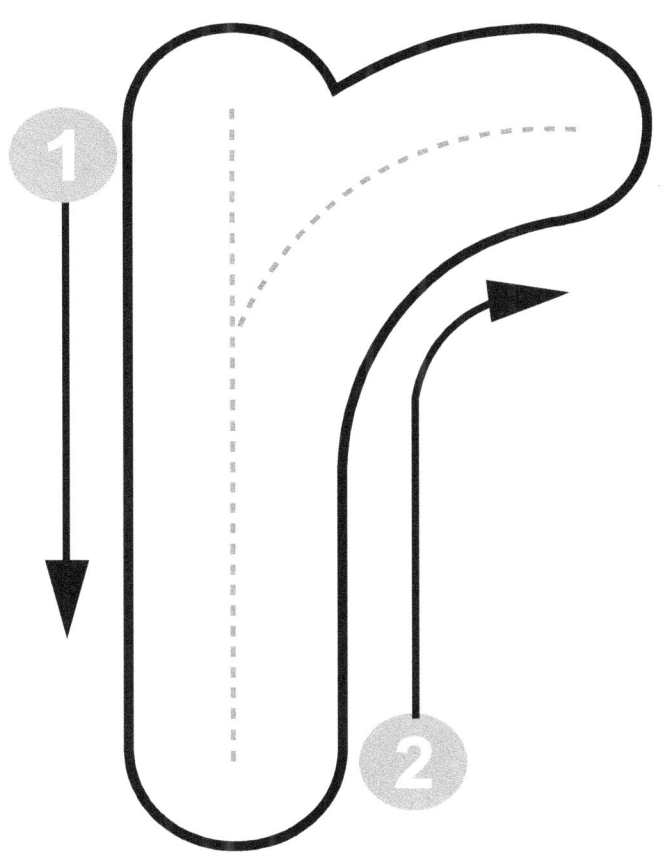

Read out loud

Rabbit

✏️ Let's trace following the numbers 📢

R R R R

Rocket

 reindeer

 Read out loud

 rain

Find every R and color them

Trace the dotted line and read out loud

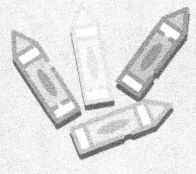 **Find every R and color the sections**

Eggadu

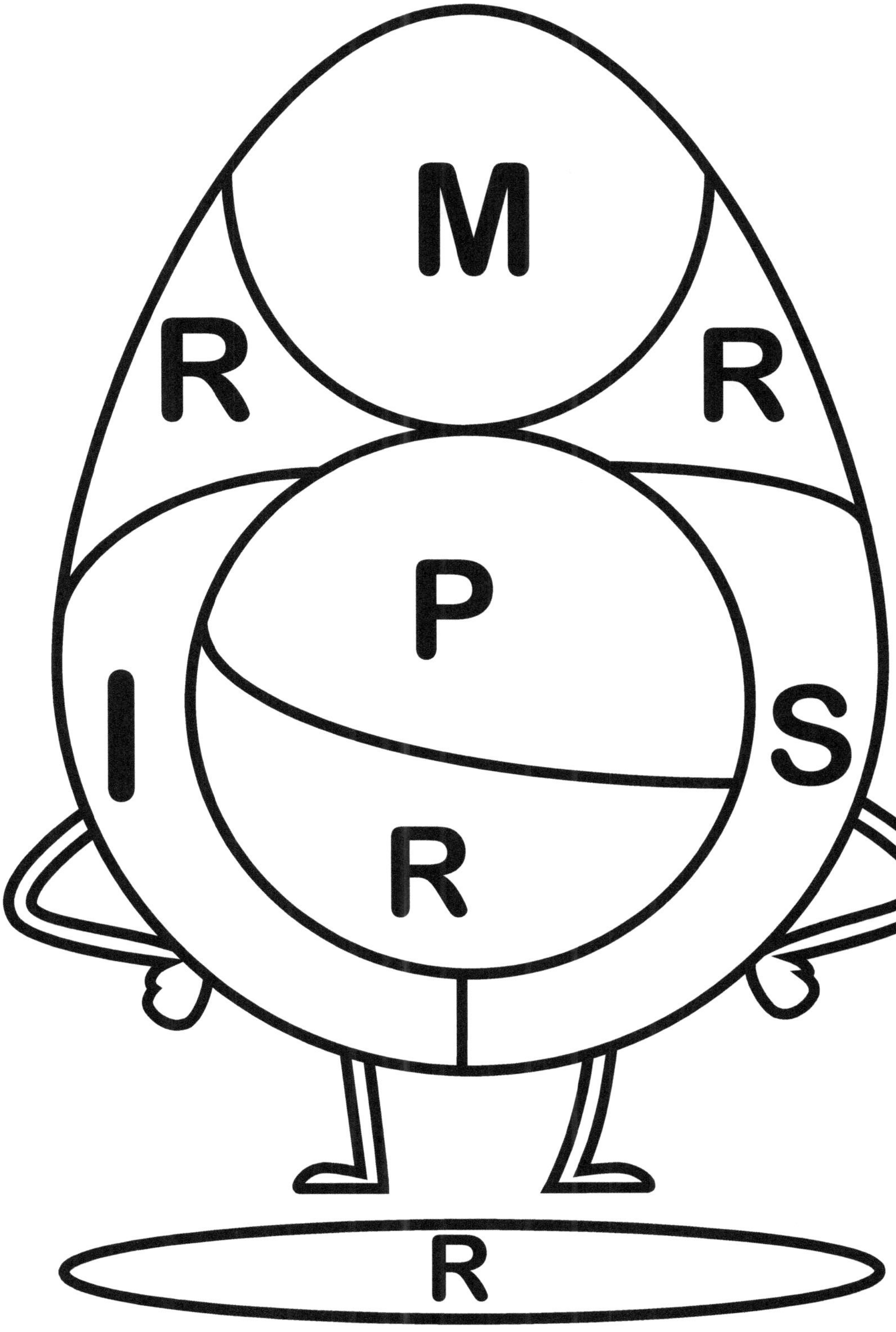

Find every r and circle them

i v
s r u u o
e x r r
r

r for rain

Trace the dotted line and read out loud

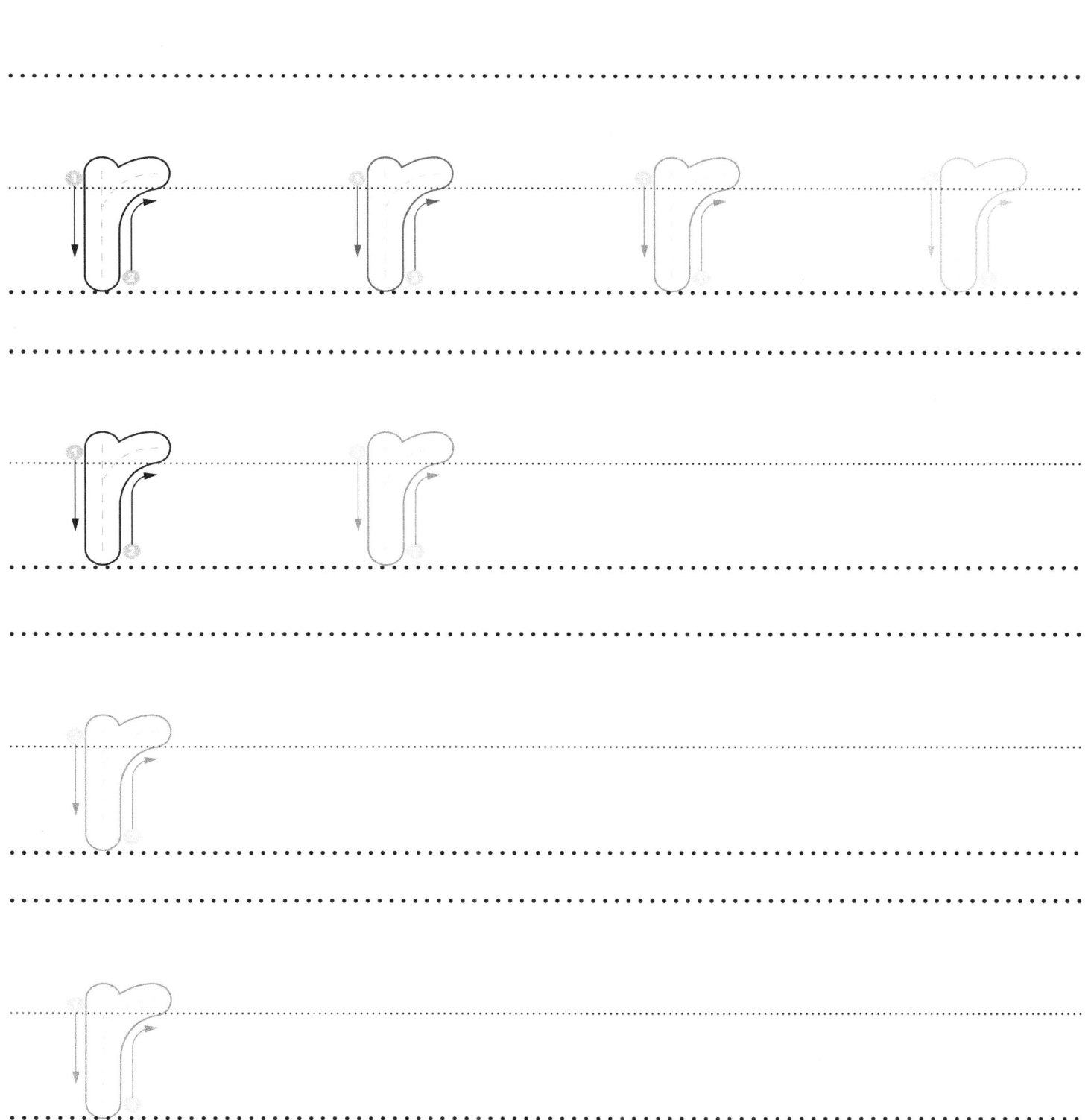

r for reindeer

Draw lines to match

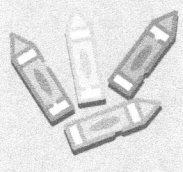 **Find every r and color the sections**

Trace the dotted line and read out loud

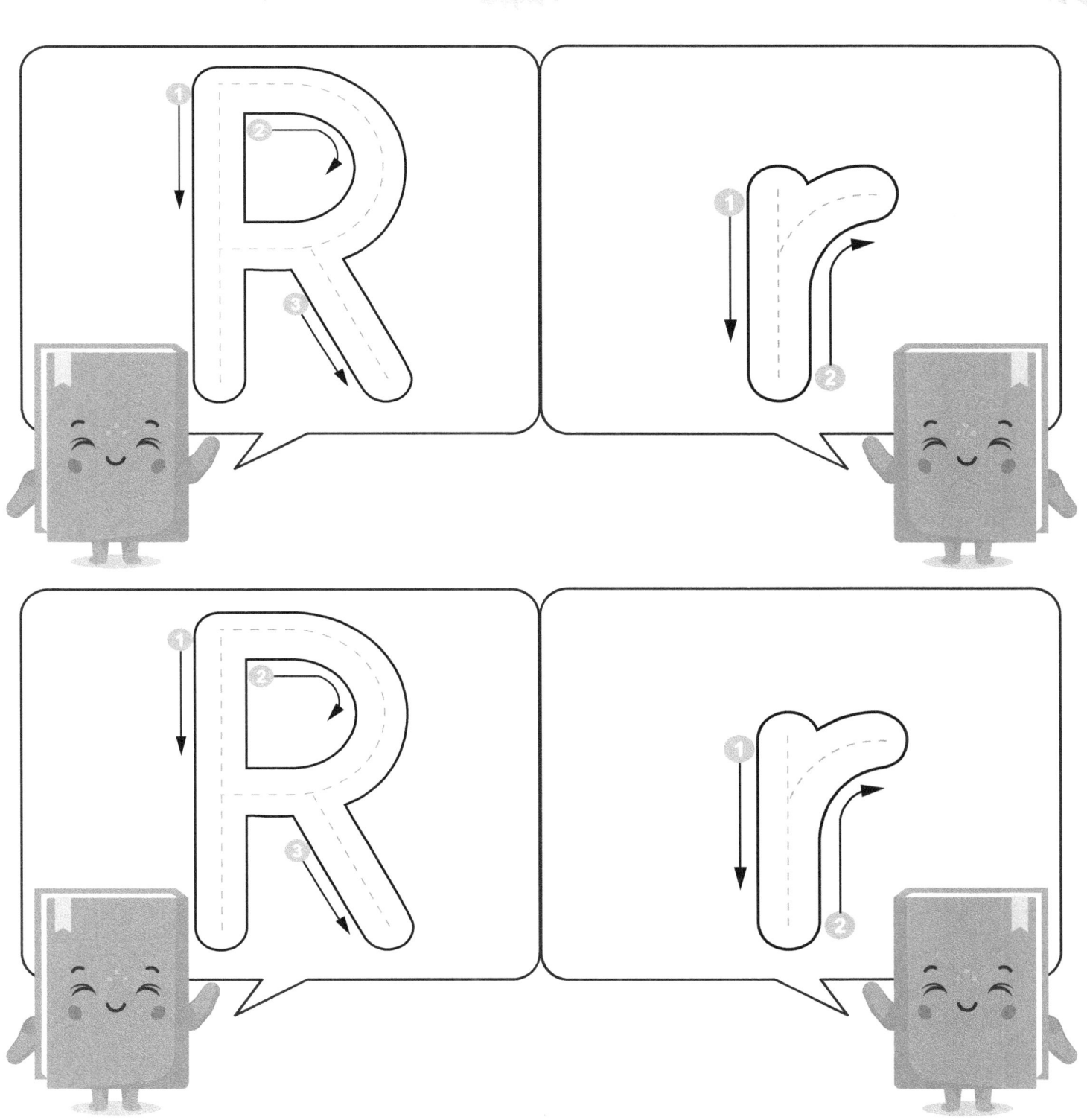

Where is Eggadu?

Find and circle!

Let's express your

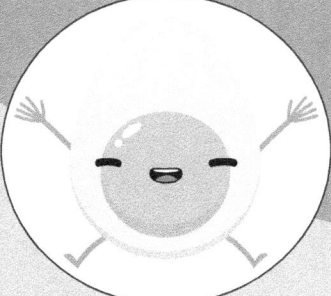

I am cool

I am hungry

I am playful

I am proud

I am okay

feelings with Eggadu!

I am tired

I am excited

I am loved

I am confident

I am happy

Let's express your

I am sad

I am calm

I am rushing

I am frustrated

I am angry

feelings with Eggadu!

I am strong

I am embarrased

I am confused

I am shy

I am brave

Write PQR and read out loud

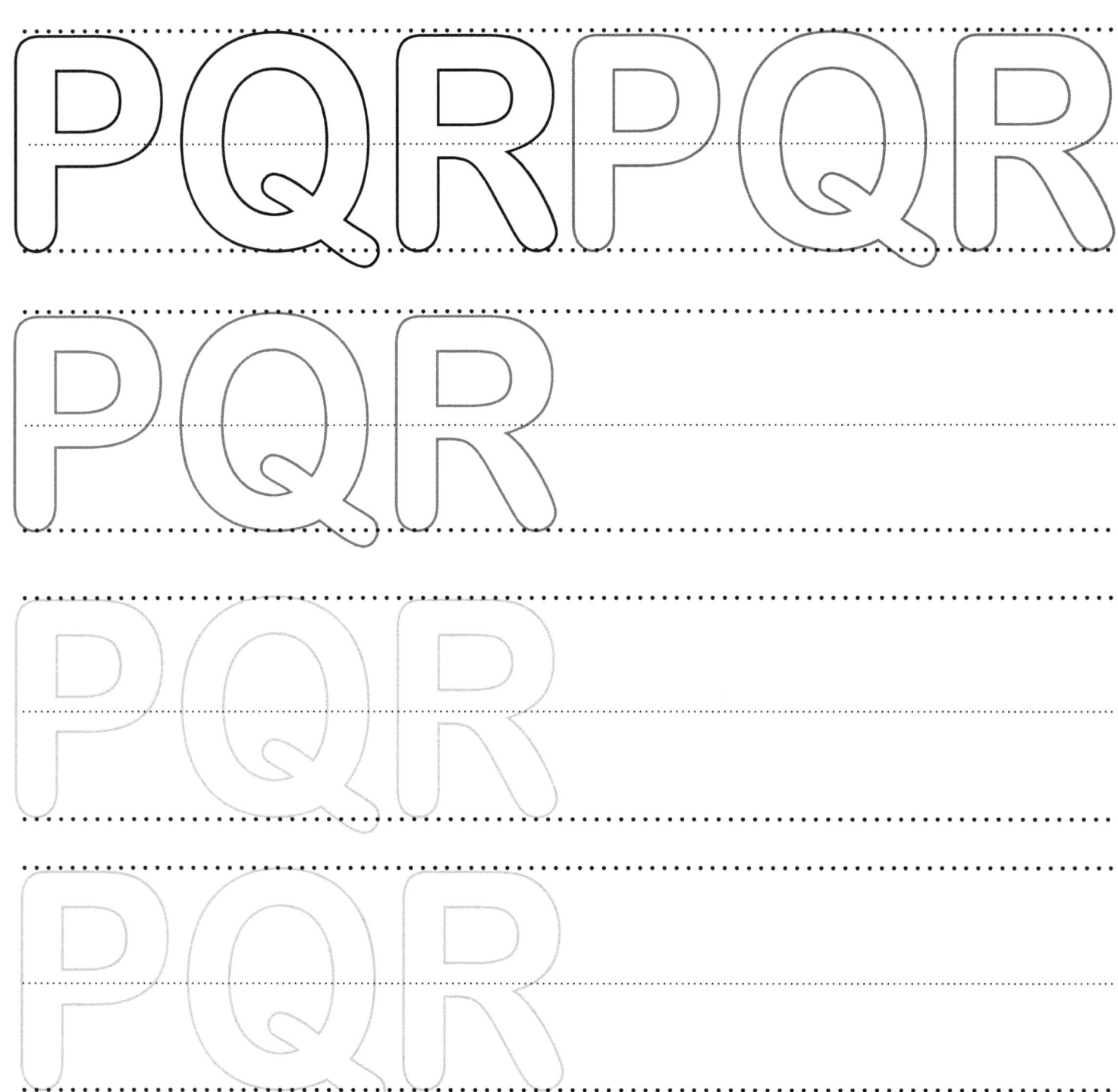

Write pqr and read out loud

Award

You are amazing!

This award is for

_____   _____
(first name)   (last name)

Great job finishing the book!

Date: _____

Visit Our Website

BigSailorEdu.com

and Get Free & Fun

Educational Material

ABC Workbook Series by Big Sailor Edu

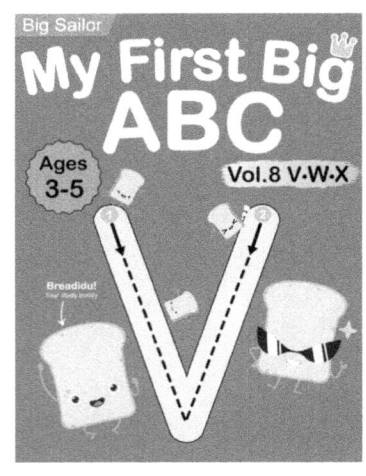

Cambridge Dynasty Press